Anonymous

The Clovers

How to sow, grow, harvest and save the seed

Anonymous

The Clovers
How to sow, grow, harvest and save the seed

ISBN/EAN: 9783337314217

Printed in Europe, USA, Canada, Australia, Japan

Cover: Foto ©Lupo / pixelio.de

More available books at **www.hansebooks.com**

The Clover

How to Sow, Grow, Harvest And Save the Seed.

Published by

Birdsell Manufacturing Co.,

South Bend, Ind.

PRICE TEN CENTS

HOW, ✗ ✗ ✗ ✗
WHEN and WHERE
TO SOW CLOVER SEED.

S the medium red and the mammoth clovers are the two varieties generally grown throughout the principal clover growing sections of the United States, we shall consider them first. We group them together for the reason that they belong to the same species, differing mainly in size of plant and time of maturing seed. Mammoth Clover, also called "pea vine," or "sappling" clover is a late maturing variety of the medium or common red clover, its season of growth being two or three weeks longer than that of the medium red. It is a very common error among farmers to regard the medium red clover as a species that yields two crops in a season, and forms seed only in the second crop, and the mammoth as a kind that produces seed in the first growth but would not yield seed in a second crop. The reas why there is, as a rule, no seed in the first crop of medium clover that its time of blossoming comes simultaneously with that of a number of other honey plants to which the Italian bees give the preference and at the season when there is a scarcity of bumble bees and hence there is lack of insect fertilization. To show that there is the true cause of the lack of the first crop of common red clover we quote from "Clover" ry Wallace, a leading authority on clover: "The con seed in the first crop wherever it has opportun We have cut on our own farms as much as from the first crop and from a thin blooms that become fertilized.

ble bees, and to the fact that during the season of first bloss
there is an abundance of preferred bloom, which prevents the l
bees from visiting the clover. Farmers have abundant proof of
fact when they cut timothy for seed, in which they find more or
clover seed when the common red is grown with timothy. T
mammoth would yield a second crop if the season were long enoug

If a mixed crop of mammoth and medium red is cut by the 15
of June, or even the 20th, and the season is favorable, many plar
of the mammoth will ripen seed, and if they are both cut by the 10
of June, a crop of seed may be expected from both. As proof of th
we cite the fact that we have mown a meadow of mixed varieties fe
ten years and the mammoth in this meadow holds its own, which i.
could not do were it not annually ripening seeds. It has never, except on one occasion been mowed prior to the 4th of July." The two
varieties of clover we have named thrive wherever limestone or calcareous soils exist, on this point Mr. Wallace says: "They grow
luxuriantly on all the limestone soils of the eastern and middle
states, and refuse to grow with a profitable luxuriance wherever the
rocks are deficient in the mineral elements peculiar to these soils.
They reach far south on the Appalachian range, and their limitation
by soil formation is most striking in Tennessee. They grow luxuriantly in middle and east Tennessee, but whenever we pass west of
the carboniferous formations into west Tennessee, they there disappear or fail to grow in desirable luxuriance. They may be found in
north Alabama and Georgia, and even far south; wherever the
peculiar geological formation of the Appalachian range appears, and
they disappear with this formation. The peculiar composition of
the drift soil that covers the prairies of most of the western states
gives these varieties a wide distribution. It is well known that most
of these soils are not made *in situ;* in other words, they are not the
results of decomposition of rocks that underlie these states, although
in many places modified by them. The drift is the result of the decomposition of rocks far distant and is mingled so thoroughly that
scarcely any section may be found in the western states in which
there is not abundance of carboniferous or calcareous matter to de-
elop a luxurious growth. The calcareous soils of the Missouri val-
y, the deposit of the calcareous formations of the upper Missouri
furnish material for the growth of clover in the greatest abundance."

Sowing Clover Seed.

S to the manner of sowing either the common red clover, or the mammoth, no rule can be given that will apply to all sections of the country, nor indeed to a very extensive area of any one section. There is more than twice as much clover seed sown each season than grows, and this waste of seed is in the main owing to the lack of study on the part of farmers as to the condition of the soil upon which it is sown, as well as the object to be achieved in sowing. Each farmer should determine by actual experiment on his own farm what manner of sowing is best adapted to his particular locality. The best known and perhaps the most successful clover farmer in the United States, Mr. T. B. Terry, of Hudson, O., prefers sowing early in the spring, when there is a light fall of snow on the ground. It is his custom to sow clover on winter wheat. In this way the seed can be seen, so there is little danger of leaving gaps or sowing double to any wide extent. By examining closely the sower can find how many seeds he is distributing on a square foot of ground. The objection to thus early sowing sometimes raised, that after germinating the young shoots may be destroyed by frost is mostly imaginary. A clover seed as long as there is any cold weather swells during the day and contracts at night, without any apparent injury. A few warm, wet days cause the seed to germinate and put out a root that catches in the porous, honey-combed soil, and the failure to get a stand of clover is by this method of sowing reduced to a minimum. There is less labor involved in this way than any other, as no harrowing is required. The alternate freezing and thawing of the ground rendering it sufficiently porous for the seeds to work downward to the proper depth to take root.

This method of sowing prevails in Kentucky and Tennessee, well as in the states north of the Ohio river, although the advantages of a snow covering for the ground at sowing time is the exception rather than the rule. The action of frost and early spring rains generally effects a sufficient covering of the seed to insure germination. Where winter wheat is used as pasture for stock, as is frequently the case in Tennessee, Virginia, Maryland and parts of Kentucky, the tramping of the animals is often relied upon to aid in covering clover seed sown in February or early March. It sometimes happens, especially in the clover growing sections south of the Ohio river that a severe frost late in March or early April will destroy a young stand of clover obtained by the above named manner of sowing.

The finest stands of clover are obtained by sowing the seed in March, on rye and pasturing off the crop with hogs, sheep or cattle. If cattle are used, only young, light stock is suitable, as the heavier animals do more damage than good by tramping too deeply, especially in wet weather. With light animals the seed is, as a rule well covered and a good stand follows. With rye as a nurse crop success is largely due to the air and sunshine that the narrow leaves of the rye do not intercept, as do the broader ones of wheat and oats.

Failure of clover when sown on winter wheat is frequently due to the hard condition of the surface of the ground, especially in a dry spring when the freezing and thawing does not, through lack of moisture render the surface sufficiently porous to imbed the seed. Where these conditions exist it is advisable to run a light harrow over the ground after sowing the clover seed and to follow it with a roller, which will compress the soil about the roots of the wheat as well as aid in properly imbedding the clover seed.

There is a large area of country in the west and north-west well adapted to the growth of clover where owing to the preponderance of spring sown grains, as well as peculiar climate conditions, especially dry windy weather, it becomes necessary to sow clover seed simultaneously with oats, barley, spring rye or spring wheat. Where this is done it becomes necessary for a fair degree of success to exercise good judgment as to the proper depth of covering the seed. Experiments made by the Agricultural College Experiment Station, at Ames, Iowa, in the spring of 1892 indicate that in a season when the rainfall is ample to insure germination clover seed may be sown at a depth varying from ½ to 3 inches without a perceptible difference as to the result. It is evident, however, that in a season when the rainfall is below normal the result would be quite different. It would then become necessary to cover the seed at the maximum depth in order to bring it in contact with the moisture in the soil; and to increase the chances of germination a heavy roller should follow the seeder, and this in turn should be followed by a light harrow, or, better still, a weeder, in order to form a mulch on the surface and keep the moisture of the lower soil from evaporating. "The most successful clover growers in the west," says Henry Wallace in the book from which we have before quoted, "and especially in the light soils of the Missouri valley, sow their clover with their spring grain and give it the same depth of covering. The almost universal custom is to cover either with the ordinary corn cultivator or the disc cultivator, which in farm practice would give clover a covering of from one-fourth of an inch to two inches."

QUANTITY OF SEED TO SOW.

WHEN it is desired to raise clover only, without an admixture of grass, 10 pounds of red or of mammoth clover seed to the acre will generally be found the proper quantity to sow. Some successful clover farmers sow only 7½ pounds to the acre—eight acres to the bushel of seed—but as a general rule 10 pounds will give the best results.

CLOVER AND TIMOTHY MIXTURE.

WHERE hay is an object as well as fall pasture 8 pounds each of timothy and clover seed should be sown. This will insure with an ordinary catch, and a fairly good growing season the year of sowing, and a favorable winter following, a good stand of clover the first year. The second year timothy will take the lead, and with an average growing season will yield an excellent hay crop, feeding as it does on the clover roots, which supply the very food the timothy thrives best upon. Mr. Wallace in "*Clover Culture*" in treating on this subject says: "Under ordinary circumstances the land should then (after taking off the timothy crop, the second year) be plowed for corn, although if it has been pastured off after the second crop has had a chance to reseed the ground the previous year, clover is apt to assert its supremacy the following year. If it does the field can be kept as a permanent meadow, in many sections at least, for an indefinite number of years, each second crop contributing its quota of seed. We have this year taken the eleventh crop from a part of a field managed in this way, and the yield has been larger, both clover and timothy than from the first year's sowing." Where it is the intention from the first to make a permanent meadow, Mr. Wallace advises that after the clover and timothy have been sown as above, orchard grass, at the rate of half a bushel per acre be sown over the same ground and harrowed in with a brush harrow. The orchard grass seed should be mixed with sand and road dust before sowing in order to insure its even distribution * * * *. The reasons for adding orchard grass to this mixture are two: First, it is about the only grass that will be fit to cut for hay at the time the common red clover is at its best estate. Second, we know of no grass, except clover, that will yield such an abundant aftermath. Where orchard grass forms any considerable portion of the sward, it should not be plowed up except after a term of years, for the reason that the seed is expensive, and the grass being a perennial or growing from year to year from the same root, should be used as long as its usefulness continues.

Where it is desired to use the clovers in connection with the other grasses as a permanent pasture, Mr. Wallace recommends a mixture as follows, provided the land has been in cultivation and it is desired to sow the grasses with spring grain.

Red clover,	5 pounds.
Mammoth clover,	5 "
Timothy,	6 "
Blue grass,	6 "
White clover,	1 "

On lands where red top thrives better than timothy, red top should be added and timothy and blue grass lessened. On wet lands Wallace recommends leaving out half the red and mammoth clovers and substituting alsike. In describing such a pasture Mr. Wallace says: "In a pasture seeded as above orchard grass will furnish the first bite, so desirable in early spring, the blue grass comes next, followed by timothy and clovers. After maturing seed the blue grass will rest while the clovers are making their most vigorous growth, but will revive and take full possession of the field when the clovers are taking time to ripen their seed crop. The disposition of blue grass and white clover to usurp full possession of permanent pastures renders it somewhat difficult to retain the red and mammoth. This difficulty may be overcome by scarifying the surface with a disc harrow and then sowing the seeds of the red and mammoth clovers, or by scattering manure containing these seeds on such pastures during the winter.

CARE OF THE GROWING PLANT.

WE do not advise turning stock on young clover the first fall after sowing. Occasionally this can be done without injury, but it is the exception, not the rule. If there is a good growth and the ground so dry that cattle do not tramp it too deeply, they may be turned into the young clover, but we prefer, if the growth is rank in the fall, to run a mower over and clip it, together with such weeds as may be in the field and the stubble remaining from the nurse crop.

In case pasture in the Spring is more needed than a crop of clover hay we would advise where the common red clover is raised that stock be turned into it as soon as the ground is sufficiently firm not to be injured by tramping, and kept upon it until about June 1st,—not later if a seed crop is sought. As soon as the stock is removed a mower should be run over the field and all such patches as are not eaten down mowed off. When a crop of hay is sought, the field should not be pastured in the Spring. We shall treat later on when to cut the hay crop, how to cure the hay, etc.

In case of mammoth clover our experience is that it should not be pastured later than June 1st, and sheep should not be turned upon it, as they eat the heart out of the plant and this prevents a paying yield of seed. The same course should be pursued with mammoth clover as with common red, i. e. a mower should be run over it as soon as the stock is taken off, to cut down such bunches of clover and such weeds as have not been eaten down.

WHEN TO CUT AND HOW TO CURE RED CLOVER FOR HAY.

AS the extent of country over which the red clover is successfully grown is very large and the climatic conditions necessarily vary greatly, and no two seasons are exactly alike no time can be named when to cut clover for hay. In northern Indiana the time varies from about the 25th of June to the 10th of July. The plant has reached its most nutritious condition when in full bloom, and this is the proper time to cut the hay crop, but as there is a difference in the time of blossoming in the central heads of the plant and the outside ones some allowance in determining the period of full bloom must be made on this account. As good a rule as any we know of, is to put the mower in the field when the first blooms are beginning to turn brown. How to properly cure clover hay is a problem as perplexing as any the farmer has to contend with. His own good judgment is perhaps the best guide. What is written annually on this subject would fill many volumns, and yet poor clover hay is the rule rather than the exception. When clover is in blossom it contains considerably more than two-thirds of its weight in moisture, the per cent being $72\frac{1}{2}$, while in its properly cured form ready for mow or stack, its water content is between 16 and 17 per cent. It becomes necessary therefore to evaporate nearly 60 per cent of moisture before it is in proper condition to go into the mow or the stack. In other words, 100 pounds of green clover, freshly cut, when in full bloom, will weigh only about 43 pounds when in proper condition for storing.

The chief problem in curing clover hay is, how to preserve the leaf of the plant intact and at the same time so cure it, that it will not be injured in the stack or mow. The preservation of the leaves is most essential for two reasons: First, their feeding value and second, their important office in evaporating the moisture from the stems, for it is through their agency that the bulk of the water content of the green clover is to find its way into the atmosphere. When there is a rank growth of clover and the swaths are necessarily heavy, the use of a tedder becomes an absolute necessity, for a heavy swath would even in the most favorable weather fail to cure properly. The upper part would become so dry that the leaves would be destroyed, and the lower part remain so green as to spoil if stored away. In no other grass is the tedder so much needed as in clover. We fully agree with Mr. Wallace, that the proper time to cut clover for hay, is in the afternoon or evening preceding the day when it is to be housed. Clover cut in this manner should be stirred with the tedder at least once the following morning, and a second stirring a little later will be all the more beneficial. With good weather it can then be put into the stack or barn the same day. Treated in this way clover hay becomes the ideal feed not only for cattle, but for horses as well, and even hogs will enjoy such a mess. There is no dust in such clover hay, neither is there woody fiber, and by thus promptly cutting the hay crop, when in full bloom, the second or seed crop will, as a general thing, be a good one.

When clover hay is dry enough to store away the stems will not exude moisture when twisted tightly. As soon as this condition is reached it should be housed with the least possible delay, for no plant when dried will absorb moisture as quickly and in such volume as clover. When once the hay has been sufficiently cured for safe housing, no time is to be lost, for whatever moisture it absorbs afterward becomes injurious to it. The farmer who raises clover largely for hay should provide himself with one of the wagon loaders now so largely used. With this a ton of hay can be put upon the wagon in considerably less than half an hour, and if he is provided with the proper unloading tools, as he should be, the work of housing becomes so expeditious that there is little excuse for having off grade clover hay, excepting only in an extremely wet season. When clover hay is stacked the stacks should always be carefully covered, preferably with slough grass, but when that is not procurable, tame hay may be used, or even straw is better than no cover. When straw is used it is necessary to fasten it on, or the winds will scatter much of it. As to the form of stack, the long rick is preferable to the round stack, as there is less surface exposed, and hence less waste.

HARVESTING AND CARING FOR THE SEED CROP.

THE clover seed crop is one of the most important products of the farm. It is one of the chief money-making crops. When rightly looked after it is perhaps, all things considered, the most profitable crop that can be raised. The first essential to success in harvesting clover seed is good judgment in the time selected for cutting; carelessness in cutting is responsible for a large share of the waste of clover seed which annually occurs. The first mistake is liable to be made in cutting the clover when it is too dry. When this is done shelling of the seed takes place to a far greater extent than seems possible to the casual observer. The cutting should always be done when the air is damp. Ordinarily a sufficient number of damp days occur to cut the crop with little loss of shelling from over dryness, but should a dry spell prevail, as is sometimes the case during the harvest time of clover seed, then it becomes necessary to cut it late at night or early in the morning. A good plan is to begin at daybreak and continue as long as there is dampness enough to be perceptible. This rule strictly adhered to will cause a saving of seed that will astonish the farmer who has been in the habit of cutting seed clover at such time as best suited his convenience, regardless of the condition of the atmosphere. The next important consideration is the machine with which seed clover should be cut. Here good judgment is again necessary in order to get the best results. The old fashioned self-rake reaper is the best of all devices for this purpose that have as yet made their appearance. The rakes permit of the proper adjustment to make the gavels or bunches of clover of the required size to suit any part of the field. The farmer who has clover to cut for seed should, by all means, have it done with a reaper whenever it is possible to do so. On farms where clover is grown for seed to any considerable extent a self-rake reaper will soon pay for itself in the saving of seed it effects. We are aware that the present self-binding grain harvester is used quite extensively; the apparatus for binding the sheaf is removed and a dropper, such as is used in harvesting flax, is substituted, but we have never seen satisfactory results by this means; not only are heads often turned downwards where this manner of cutting is employed, but the clover lodges against the cutter bar, and instead of all being caught by the reel and delivered on the platform apron a part remains in an upright position against the cutter bar until the sickle cuts it up and drops it to the ground.

The common grass mower is also used for cutting seed clover, but this manner of cutting should never be resorted to except, perhaps, in a light stand badly mixed with weeds. In raking the swath after the mower there is always an unavoidable waste of seed. When reapers were high priced we have frequently seen an improvised table or platform attached to a mower to let the clover accumulate until there was enough to make a fair sized gavel, when a man raked it off the platform with a hand rake. This plan is not worth considering now, when a reaper can be bought for less than half the price mowers were sold at a few years ago.

HOW TO GET CLOVER SEED OF STRICTLY PRIME QUALITY AND COLOR.

THE difference in the market value of clover seed raised in Wisconsin or in Kentucky and Tennessee is wholly owing to the respective differences in cutting and handling the clover afterward. In Wisconsin it is not cut until ripe. The heads are permitted to turn black before the reaper enters the field, while in the south the habit of cutting early, when the heads are only brown, is the rule. When seed clover is cut too early there is a green tinge to the seed, which it retains even though it is afterward handled in the best possible manner. It is essential, therefore, that the heads should become black before the clover is cut. The fact that the plant is permitted to thoroughly ripen before being cut does not necessarily subject it to waste of seed in the process of cutting, if the proper care is taken to cut only when the air is sufficiently damp to do the best work. The greater loss from shelling in thoroughly ripe clover is much more than compensated for in the additional value of the seed over that of clover cut too early. To get strictly prime seed, plump and possessing the purple color characteristic of the best Wisconsin seed, it is essential that the gavels should lie in the field a sufficient length of time for the straw to become at least partially rotten. There is no danger of injury by rains unless they are too protracted, when sprouting of seed is liable to occur, but up to the point of sprouting the gavels may remain in the field before being taken to the huller, if turned occasionally to prevent sprouting. When this plan is followed seed of the choicest quality and color will be the result. The grower of clover seed should never permit it to be hulled, in any ordinary season, before it has had at least one good rain, and several rains will not injure it, provided no water stands on the ground, and care is taken to turn the gavels or bunches afterward. The action of the rain not only renders the separation of the seed from the pod in the process of hulling easier, but it is the chief agent in imparting to the seed the purple color seed buyers regard as its most desirable feature.

THRESHING, HULLING AND CLEANING CLOVER SEED.

TO prepare clover for the huller, the gavels should be turned the day before the huller is to do the work. Only a careful hand should do this. A wide fork should be used, and the turning so gently done that no seed will be threshed out by the operation. To haul the clover to the huller a low wagon is best, or, if there is no such wagon to be had, a sleigh can be used, as the clover will have become so light that the weight of the loads as usually carried is insignificant. The gavels, or bunches of clover should be taken up by running the fork under them and laid very carefully upon the rack of the wagon or sleigh used for hauling them to the huller. In pitching from the loaded vehicle to the huller the same care must be exercised as in loading, or seed will be wasted at this stage.

WHAT STYLE OF HULLER TO USE.

THERE is nothing more important in successful clover seed raising than the matter of hulling and cleaning the seed. The farmer who is not fully posted as regards the hulling of clover is very liable to sustain serious loss after all the work of raising, harvesting and caring for the crop is over; in the very last and most expensive operation to which it is subjected. The first thing to be avoided is the so-called clover hulling attachments to grain threshers. It is impossible to get even the larger portion of the seed out of the straw with such attachments, and the little that is threshed out and saved is so poorly cleaned as to necessitate passing it through a cleaning mill; and after all this is done, there is usually a large per cent. of broken seed to be found in the debris of the fanning mill, which was broken in passing the clover through the "attachment." Little better than the threshing machine "attachment" is the clover huller with a spike hulling cylinder and concaves. Such a machine always has been and always will be a decided failure. It is an impossibility to arrange either spikes or nails in a hulling cylinder and its concaves in such a manner as to rub all of the seed out of the pods of the clover plant. Time and again have threshermen who owned rasp hullers rethreshed the chaff and straw after a spike machine, and obtained more seed than the spike huller got out of it at the first hulling. The thresherman who is posted on clover hulling will not buy nor use a spike huller, and the farmer who is "at himself" will not permit it to hull his clover, or rather to hull at it; for at best it hulls only a part of the seed out of it. Not only are the hullers with either spikes or nails in their hulling cylinders and concaves defective at that most essential point, but the separating devices in them are, as a rule, quite as defective as the hulling cylinder. To do the best work in hulling clover there must be a picker behind the threshing cylinder to tear the clover apart; where this is lacking, as is always the case with spike hullers, the clover, as it comes from the threshing cylinder, will go through the machine in a more or less bunched condition, instead of traveling in a uniform mass, as it should do, and when even the smallest bunch reaches the rear end of the rakes it carries more or less seed into the straw pile with it. But the lack of a picker in a spike huller is only one defective point. The rakes, which are moved by multiple cranks, travel between slats, and in doing so permit a large amount of broken straw, weeds, etc., to drop through and lodge upon the conveyer table below, and thus enter the hulling cylinder, where, at a considerable expense of power, they are ground or broken up, and thus go to the shoe to be either blown over the tail board of the machine or they enter the tailings spout or conveyer and are elevated back into the machine, and this operation is repeated over and over again. The reason that all spike hullers choke so persistently is that by their process of separating they necessarily load up every part of the machine with the broken straw, weed stems, etc., and therefore continually overwork separating parts, hulling cylinder and shoe. The principles involved in the construction of the spike huller are wrong from the separating parts to and including the hulling cylinder, and they cannot therefore do good work anywhere or in any condition of clover. Every thresherman who has run one knows what the choking of the hulling cylinder in such a machine means. When it occurs a lever and chain is usually resorted to for the purpose of working the cylinder back and forth, and thus loosening up the impacted mass that has lodged between the teeth. If this fails there is nothing to do but remove the upper cylinder and other adjacent parts and burrow down into the hulling cylinder, which means hours of hard work for himself and idleness of the balance of the crew. In the spike huller the concave is necessarily stationary, and it is therefore impossible to prevent choking of the machine. Some of the makers of such machines aware of this very serious defect have made the lower concave of the hulling cylinder so that three staves can be taken out, but this fails to remedy the matter materially, for the reason that there are thirteen rows of concave teeth choked at the time, and the removal of three of these leaves ten as firmly impacted as before the three staves were taken out. The owner or operator of one of these machines is continually between the " devil and the deep sea." The only way he can keep his machine from choking is to lower the tail board, and when this is done seed is continually blown over; then he is compelled to raise it, and this causes choking. Compare such a machine as above described with

THE RASP HULLER,

MADE by the Birdsell Manufacturing Company, South Bend, Ind., with its picker just back of the threshing cylinder, its vibrating tables or bolts, whereon a perfect separation of the heads from the stalks takes place, the heads alone falling through and being carried by a conveyer floor to the hulling cylinder, which, together with its concave, is completely covered over with steel rasp; the concave being adjustable to exactly the proper distance for every size and every condition of clover seed, its roomy tailings, elevator capable of elevating all that can possibly come to it, a shoe that never needs attention when the machine is run at proper speed, its fan that gives just the proper degree of wind, its perfect recleaner that cleans seed ready for any market, its sixteen-foot jointed folding stacker, or its light running wind stacker, and its automatic feeder, and then judge for yourself as to the machine that is needed wherever clover is grown.

THERE IS NO OTHER HULLER

THAT in any essential feature resembles the Birdsell. It is the only huller employing rasp for rubbing clover seed from the pods. The hulling cylinder is entirely covered with rasp and its concave lined with it. This rasp is made of extra hardened steel, which makes it durable and renders it proof against injury from such trash as often passes through a huller. The Birdsell is the only clover huller made that elevates the tailings toward the rear of the machine, and empties them on the conveyer floor, which takes them direct to the hulling cylinder. The spike hullers either empty them in front of the hulling cylinder (where the feeder gets the full benefit of the dust), or into one end of the hulling cylinder; thus giving that end of the cylinder more work to do than the other, detracting just so much from its already overtaxed capacity for good work. It is a notorious fact that all spike hullers require much larger engines or horse powers than does the Birdsell rasp huller.

There is a difference in favor of the Birdsell rasp huller of full four-horse power. The Birdsell huller, equipped with wind stacker and automatic feeder, does not require an engine of more than ten-horse power, and it can be run successfully with an eight-horse power engine. The Birdsell wind stacker does not need more than half as much power as other makes of wind stackers. It has two fans about one-half the circumference of those used in other wind stackers, and hence the power required to run it is reduced to the minimum.

No thresherman who has ever owned and operated a rasp huller will use a spike machine afterward, and no farmer who has had experience with both styles of machines will permit any save the rasp huller to do his work. From one-third to one-half more seed will be obtained by the rasp huller than by the spike machine, and it should be borne in mind always that there is only one rasp huller made, and that one is the Birdsell.

ALFALFA OR LUCERNE.

NATURE has provided some species of *Leguminosæ* for nearly every climate and almost every variety of soil. There is a western line where, owing to the lack of rainfall, red clover either does not grow at all, or at its best is unprofitable, and this line seems to be the meeting point of the red clover and the alfalfa. And what is true in this regard of the west is likewise true of the south. Alfalfa is at its best in California and New Mexico, wherever irrigation is practiced and it extends southward into Central and South America and seems to thrive over a like extent of south latitude. On our own Pacific coast it is the one successful hay and pasture plant. In the valleys of Colorado it again appears as the standard grass. It follows the valley of the Arkansas river from Colorado into Kansas, where its range is gradually extending toward the red clover line. In Nebraska it is likewise spreading rapidly and is also on the increase in Texas. We have for some years past watched carefully the efforts to raise alfalfa in the red clover area, and the progress made is not sufficient to justify us in recommending it wherever the red clover, alsike or crimson clovers can be grown with any reasonable degree of success. It requires much more labor in the preparation of the seed bed, and unless the subsoil is sufficiently porous for the roots to penetrate and find the large amount of water the plant requires it will not do well and indeed, as a general rule it entirely disappears in the course of from two to three seasons. The farmers in the red clover area who have succeeded in getting alfalfa to grow successfully are very few and their experience with the hay has on the whole been unsatisfactory. Alfalfa, to make the best hay or indeed to make hay fit to feed must be cut when about one-fourth of the blossoms are out, or it becomes woody; and as this is precisely the time when it is full of sap, it is extremely difficult to cure it properly in the red clover "belt." Where red clover thrives the air contains too much moisture to properly cure alfalfa hay. Where the soil is saturated with water alfalfa invariably dies out, nor does it survive where it is covered with ice during a part of the winter. The following excerpt from Professor Georgeson's experience, as related in his contribution to Henry Wallace's "Clover Culture," from which we have before quoted, is appropos, "There are places where alfalfa cannot grow, regardless of climate. Wherever there is an impervious clay, the so called 'gumbo,' or a layer of hard-pan, or rock within a few feet of the surface, it will be a total failure if on the uplands, and but a very indifferent success on the bottom lands. Likewise on the bottom lands, where the soil water stands too near the surface, or where it is overflowed for considerable periods, alfalfa should not be sown." The same author in the same publication recommends alfalfa for not only the valleys in Kansas where irrigation is practiced, but for both the unirrigated bottom lands and even for the uplands of that state. In this connection he says: "Actual trials in many places have demonstrated that alfalfa can be grown on these dry uplands, but the yield in forage is not to be compared with the yield in the lowlands. In the first place the obtaining of a good stand is attended with more difficulties. If the rain in the early part of May is sufficient only to germinate the seed, but not enough to sustain the young plants till they get a foothold, the stand will be light, and at times it may require two or three seedings before the crop is well started. Again, the growth the first year is feeble, and nothing either in the way of pasture or hay can reasonably be expected from it the first season; no pasture, because it would kill the crop to turn the stock on it, and no hay because the growth is too light. The second, third and succeeding years it will yield increasingly good pasture, but it is only in favorable seasons that it will produce fair hay crops under the conditions named. It is, however, a great thing for the plant to live and yield pasturage, for as pasturage it far exceeds the wild grasses both in quantity and quality. There is no better pasture for horses, hogs and sheep, nor indeed for cattle, except that it sometimes causes them to bloat. This upland alfalfa has one other good feature—it yields seed of superior quality, even though only in moderate quantity. Combining these features—good pasturage, an occasional hay crop and a sure producer of good seed—and to add to this its manurial properties which is by no means its least virtue, we have in alfalfa a better forage plant for the western plains than any other perennial that has yet been brought to our notice."

SOWING ALFALFA SEED.

THE first essential in the culture of alfalfa is to prepare the seed bed. The ground may be plowed either in the fall or early in the spring, the same depth as for oats or wheat. Repeated harrowings should be given the land on which the seed is to be sown, and if there are any lumps it will be well to pass a roller over it after the harrowing is done. The ground should be sufficiently moist when the seed is sown to insure its germination. Where there is lack of moisture it should be irrigated before the seed is sown. The seed may be sown either broadcast or in drills. It should be covered about one inch deep. The amount of seed to the acre should be from 20 to 25 pounds. Alfalfa does not do well when sown with a nurse crop; those who are most successful with it give it the full use of the ground. Where irrigation is possible the first wetting, after the young plants are started, should take place as soon as the plants are seen to be well above ground. This first watering of the young plants must be done with great care in order to prevent injury. Care must be taken to prevent washing away of the soil and consequent covering up of the young growth. It is customary in the valleys where irrigation prevails to give the crop from two to three waterings before the first cutting, the first one when the plant first appears, the second a few weeks later and the third just before cutting, i. e., long enough before to let the ground dry sufficiently for mowing and curing the hay. A difference of opinion prevails as to this last watering. Some prefer to wait until the first crop is cut and housed, and then let the water on immediately after. The field is always irrigated at least once between each cutting, and occasionally twice. Where a seed crop is desired it follows the first cutting. It is seldom the case that a profitable hay crop can be cut the same season after a seed crop, but good pasturage follows the seed crop and lasts through the season. A good crop of alfalfa will yield from 2½ to 3 tons of hay at the first cutting, and the seed crop that follows will be from 6 to 8 bushels per acre. When no seed crop is wanted and hay only is sought, the field can under favorable conditions be mowed from 5 to 6 times, and the average will be about four cuttings in a season on the Pacific coast. In Colorado and Kansas the average is about three cuttings. The yield of hay from an acre of thrifty alfalfa is from five to eight tons a season.

HULLING ALFALFA SEED.

IN the alfalfa plant the seed is encased in a pod which terminates in a hard, sharp-pointed horn. This horn must be broken by the machine employed to do the hulling in order to get the seed out of it. This being the case, it becomes evident at once that no spike huller can possibly do good work in alfalfa. The Birdsell rasp huller is the only hulling machine in the world built expressly for alfalfa. It is sold under the positive guarantee that it will get all the seed out of the straw and save it. In hulling alfalfa the amount of tailings to be elevated is much greater than in common clover, and the elevator in the Birdsell huller has been constructed with that end in view. It is capable of taking care of all that comes to it without ever clogging. It elevates toward the rear of the machine, the same as on the clover huller, and dumps the tailings on the conveyer floor, from where they go direct to the hulling cylinder. In most other hullers the tailings are taken to the entrance of the threshing cylinder, where the feeder gets the full benefit of the enormous amount of dust the alfalfa contains. The large yield of seed in alfalfa, as compared with common red clover, necessitates increased capacity in the recleaner, which has been fully provided for in the Birdsell alfalfa huller. The upper separating bolt or vibrating table in the Birdsell alfalfa huller differs from the one in the clover machine, as does also the shape of the deck, and the length of the threshing cylinder, which in the alfalfa machine is 36 inches. The axles and wheels for the alfalfa machines are made from the most carefully selected stock, and are warranted to stand the wear and tear to which they are subject in the western alfalfa region. The new wind stacker and the automatic feeder are attached to the alfalfa machines, as well as to the ordinary clover huller. Readers of this pamphlet who have alfalfa to hull should write to Birdsell Manufacturing Company, South Bend, Ind., for huller catalogue.

HOW AND WHEN TO SOW AND RAISE ALSIKE CLOVER.

ALSIKE or Swedish clover is far too little known or cultivated. Its value in the utilization of wet lands makes it a favorite wherever known. It thrives where few other tame grasses can be raised, and yields an abundance of the best of all clover hay. Mr. Wallace in "Clover Culture" recommends it particularly for sowing about the edges of sloughs, and states that good results are obtained " by burning the slough grass off in the fall, and sowing the alsike seed in the following March, and afterward either pasturing the grass off or otherwise, early in June cutting down the grass, with a mower, in order to secure light and air for the young plants, and the grass and clover together can be mown in the fall as a grass crop. The next year unless the land or the season be very wet but little will remain save the alsike, which may be used either as a hay crop or for seed. The effect of seeding in this manner," continues Mr.Wallace, " will be somewhat surpris. ing. On wet lands where the coarser varieties of slough grass grow, the growth of the alsike will be accompanied by the decay of the roots of the coarser grasses, they being smothered out by the rank growth of the alsike. This will have the effect in time of allowing the water to sink away that has heretofore been held by the mass of the roots of the wild grass, and especially if the land be pastured after the first and second year's mowing, the entire surface will be compacted by the tramping of cattle, and if a slough the water confined to the center. It will then be possible in the course of two or three years to sow white or red clover or blue grass, the result of drier conditions. In fact, we know of no way of reaucing the width of a slough and limiting it to a narrow channel, so effectively as sowing with alsike and treating in the manner above indicated." Alsike clover is a perennial. The stalk is more slender than in the red clover, but as it grows thicker on the ground, the yield of forage compares favorably with that of the common red, while the seed yield is somewhat in excess of the red. The size of the seed is between that of the white clover and the common red. It is easily distinguished by its difference in color, the alsike seed being of a greenish hue. The seed always commands a good price, averaging as a rule about six dollars per bushel, and seldom falling below four dollars. Alsike is not often cut for hay, except when it is mixed with other grasses. It is more of a pasture plant, but its value lies chiefly in the seed crop, its fertilizing qualities and its adaptability to low land, where few of the tame grasses can be grown. It is very popular in northwestern Ohio, especially in Williams and Defiance counties, and is rapidly spreading in Wood, Henry and Putnam counties. It never fails to become a favorite on lands that are moist and not underdrained, and where it is most largely raised, farm mortgages are few.

HULLING ALSIKE CLOVER.

THERE is only one clover huller that can be used to hull alsike and that one is the Birdsell rasp huller. The spike hullers do poor enough work in any clover, but in alsike they simply do not work at all. The Birdsell clover huller is warranted to get all the alsike seed out of the straw and save it, and to clean the seed ready for market. The alsike farmer cannot afford to fool away time and money in experimenting with clover hullers. The spike hullers would be dear property as a gift to the alsike grower. The Birdsell hul'er as adjusted for red clover does perfect work in alsike, the only alteration required being a finer screen in the recleaner, made expressly for alsike seed.

SCARLET, OR CRIMSON CLOVER.

SCARLET, or crimson clover thrives best near the Atlantic coast from the northern boundary of New Jersey to the northern line of South Carolina. It does well on both the sandy soils of the coast lands and the white clays. It is grown more or less in every southern state, from Florida to Texas, but nowhere else does it grow as well nor bear as large a yield of seed as in New Jersey, Delaware, Maryland and North Carolina. North of the Ohio river and west of the Allegheny mountains crimson clover is liable to winter kill unless it has some protection. Those who have succeeded in getting good results in northern Indiana have sown it in growing corn and left the corn stalks standing in the field over winter. With this protection good crops of seed, averaging eight bushels per acre have been raised. We are, however, inclined to the belief that where common red, mammoth and alsike clovers thrive these had best be adhered to as a general rule. There are, however, times when crimson clover may be sown to advantage at the last cultivation of some hoed crop and be plowed under either late in the fall or early following spring to good advantage even as far north as southern Iowa. We shall therefore deal somewhat at length with it, and reproduce a part of a supplement issued with the "Clover Leaf" in December, 1892. The following description we reproduce from the XVI. Bulletin of the Delaware College Agricultural Experiment Station, of which Arthur T. Neale is director:

I.

A DESCRIPTION OF THE PLANT, AND ITS COMPARISON WITH ORDINARY RED CLOVER.

Scarlet clover is an annual. About the first week in June it can be expected to mature a crop of seed, from sowings made during the preceding July, August and September. If pastured in the early spring it renews its growth, in part at least, and matures at the usual time. It may be seeded in April, a practice followed in central and southern Europe whenever it is to be used as a substitute, for red clover crops, ruined by severe winters. This plan has been attempted once at least by this Station; a May sowing gave a very heavy growth during the following fall, but no blossoms appeared and the plants were destroyed during the winter by a fungus, harbored under the excessive forage. It is a rank grower at one stage of its development; stools to an unusual degree when opportunity offers; attains oftentimes to a height of two feet; is characterized by a brilliant scarlet blossom, will easily yield per acre eight tons of green fodder if cut between the fifth and tenth of May; roots to the depth of two feet even in unfavorable soil; and for silage, hay, and to plow down for green manure compares well, under favorable conditions, with any leguminous crop.

In comparison with ordinary red clover, its most marked peculiarities are:

1. Its ability to flourish on relatively poor soil.
2. Its development during the fall, winter and spring.

Growing at a time of year when most of our foul weeds are in seed, it escapes one danger, and provided with an unusually well developed root system it finds sufficient food when red clover would be on half rations.

As it grows when wheat and even rye seem dormant, scarlet clover can not be seeded with winter grain. One or the other crop would be destroyed.

As it is in blossom on or about May 1, it can be used for many purposes other than those usually served by red clover, particularly for soiling and for plowing down in place of rye.

II.

SEED.

Of the five varieties of this clover known to European writers four have scarlet blossoms and differ from each other essentially in their relative powers to withstand winter weather. In that respect the original seed supply on this peninsula seems, fortunately, to have been of the sturdiest type. The fifth variety is characterized by a white flower, which in shape and size is practically identical with that of the true scarlet forms.

Many a field in Kent county has furnished a few fine specimens of this white blossoming plant, but to the best of my knowledge it has never attracted attention enough to cause its peculiarities to be studied. One thought, however, is awakened by the color of its blossom, viz.: Schmedlin, in his valuable treatise on the leguminous plants of Germany, calls attention to a falsification of scarlet clover seed. He states that the Egyptian clover *Trifolium Alexandrinum* yields more seed than any known variety. This seed so closely resembles scarlet clover seed that one reliable seedsman was misled by it and in turn misled his customers.

A peculiarity of the Egyptian clover is a white blossom. It differs decidedly, however, in shape and size from that of the scarlet types. It is valuable in very many respects, but it is a *summer clover* and can not stand late frosts, to which it might be exposed if seeded early in the spring. Much less certain is it to mature a crop if handled as our scarlet variety is handled and should be handled.

The prevailing tone among the writers who represent the

COMMON RED CLOVER. (*Trifolium pretense.*)

northern section of the United States is, that scarlet clover "winters out." Is it certain that in every unfavorable case, scarlet clover has been under test? May not the abundant crops of Egyptian clover seed have been substituted and passing innocently through importers' hands, may they not have reached consumers, and thus have given good ground apparently for the unfavorable verdict? Certain it is that the Delaware type of scarlet clover has stood low temperatures when seeded upon any proper soil on this peninsula.

One other doubtful point is here brought to the attention of conservative farmers:

The annual report of this station for the year 1890 shows that a disease, well known in Germany and France under the name of clover cancer, but hitherto unknown in the United States, made its appearance upon three of this station's experimental plots at Newark. The seed used is believed to have been from imported stock. This disease attacks and destroys —red clover, white clover. scarlet clover and alsike clover. One method only for securing relief from its ravages is noted by those who have had experience with it, that is, *to avoid the cultivation of clover crops for a term of years.* Now it is possible that the fungus, which Professor Chester identified as the true cause of this cancer, may exist in the United States, harboring upon other crops or upon weeds. Possibly it has already caused losses in clover fields which have never been understood because the attention of men who are especially skilled in detecting the causes of such trouble has not been attracted. But, one thing is evident, the liability to meet this disease may be lessened by selecting seed grown under one's own eyes upon fields known to be free from the clearly visible manifestations of this fungus.

III.

WHEN, WHERE AND HOW TO SOW SCARLET CLOVER SEED.

It has been established by several years' experience that an excellent "take" of scarlet clover can be secured from seedings in peach, pear and apple orchards, provided the seed is sown immediately after the last cultivation of the trees—

MAMMOTH CLOVER. (*Trifolium medium.*)

that is, about the middle of July. Seedings in August have also been thoroughly successful.

A very large acreage in field corn in Delaware is also seeded each year to scarlet clover immediately after the cultivation of this crop is finished for the season. If the corn is an ordinary crop, check rowed, then success in securing a "catch" is the rule and the crop is unusually heavy in growth, but if drilled and cultivated in one direction only, then a possibility of a poor "catch" exists. If pumpkin seeds are planted with the corn, a good "take" of clover may be seriously damaged by the vines.

Any field from which early crops have been removed may be seeded. Success with millet and with buckwheat as *cover crops* have been reported. One failure where the millet was unusually heavy has been noted.

The quantity of seed to be used depends upon the aims of the sower. It varies between five and fifteen pounds per acre. In orchards and in standing corn the Cahoon broadcaster is a very serviceable machine. With it an energetic man can seed four acres per hour in corn, by walking in one middle and seeding two others on either hand, thus covering ten middles in one round trip. Seeding from horseback is also practiced, the casts in this case being made by hand.

As to the necessity of covering the seed, opinions differ widely, successes and failures being freely credited to and charged against each method.

Failures in securing a stand are most frequently charged by practical men to heavy beating rains, closely following the day of seeding. As one eminent southern writer expresses it however, the damage is generally caused by the intense heat of the sun following the rain storm and falling upon the sprouting seed.

ALFALFA. (*Medicago sativa.*)

SCARLET CLOVER AS A CROP TO PLOW DOWN FOR GREEN
MANURE.

a. In peach, pear and apple orchards.

b. For corn crops, for potatoes and for tomatoes.

Any growing crop which occupies the ground during September, October and November, preserves the valuable nitrates, which, according to Lawes and Gilbert, would be washed into the subsoil or drains if fields lie in the condition usually seen in corn growing countries. Of all crops for this purpose the clover excels, for if the available nitrates in the ground are not sufficient for its development, then a leguminous plant like the clover, as Hellriegal and Atwater have demonstrated, can take care of itself, having the peculiar power of securing its nitrogen indirectly from the air.

To make the chain complete, practical men report that scarlet clover decays, under ground, far more rapidly than other varieties familiar in Delaware agriculture, and by decaying liberates its stores of nitrogen, phosphoric acid and potash for the use of any crops which may follow in the rotation.

SCARLET CLOVER IN PEACH, PEAR AND APPLE ORCHARDS.

In no other place in Delaware farm management has the scarlet clover found a better or more useful field than in the orchards. Where land is very poor, capable of producing ten bushels of corn only per acre, there a heavy burden of green matter can be plowed under in May. The custom has arisen to turn the sod in such a manner that many of the blossoms remain above ground. In time, seed ripens; by harrowing the land, this seed is scattered, and a very heavy crop of clover soon begins to grow therefrom. This method of seeding involves no expense whatever.

When the soil in a peach or pear orchard has been enriched so that it could raise twenty bushels of corn per acre, then practical men advise caution. Messrs. E. H. Bancroft and J. G. Brown fill their silos with clover from their orchards; Col. E. L. Martin and Charles Wright make clover hay. In both cases, relatively broad strips, uncut on either side of the rows

ALSIKE. (*Trifolium hybridum.*)

are left and after the orchard has been plowed and cultivated, the matured seed from these strips, drifting in the wind or purposely scattered by the owner, insure a heavy catch of clover for the following season. By thus removing the largest proportion of the clover, respect is shown for the opinion that too much nitrogen aids in the destruction of peach trees by yellows and of pear trees by fire blight.

SCARLET CLOVER PLOWED DOWN FOR CORN, POTATOES AND TOMATOES.

AS already stated, seed for this clover must be sown in July or August. In order therefore to use this crop to enrich a cornfield, in ordinary rotation, fall pasture of meadows or mowed field must be given up and a substitute found for food consumed in August, September and October. This will be found in the pasture afforded later by the clover, and in the turnip crop which can be raised with it. From seed sown in July or early August a heavy crop of clover can be plowed under as early as the first week in May. If the custom prevails of allowing a second corn crop to follow the first, then as soon as the first crop is "laid by" in July, seed at once to scarlet clover using twelve pounds of seed per acre. This will afford late winter and early spring pasture during the following year and will be fit to plow down in good season for the second corn planting.

Exact experiments made at Dover, Del., give a high valuation to scarlet clover when plowed under for a sweet potato crop. As a substitute for nitrate of soda, in raising that crop, it was a decided success. On Irish potatoes, planted late, it promises also to be of advantage. In two cases tested by this station the results were good, although extraordinary yields were not obtained.

3

SCARLET OR CRIMSON CLOVER.(*Trifolium incarnatum.*)

SCARLET CLOVER FOR SILAGE.

CUTTING the crop green in quantities sufficient for each day's supply is also coming into use. One writer in the *Country Gentleman* represents that farmers in the neighborhood of Richmond, Va., find it profitable to send loads of the fresh clover to the city and retail it to liverymen for ten cents per heaping bushel basket.

SCARLET CLOVER FOR HAYMAKING.

THE first and second weeks in May seem rather early for haymaking, yet good crops of scarlet clover were successfully cured last year, at that time by a number of farmers. Whether this can be done every year remains to be seen. In quality this hay may be of the highest. Analyses made at this station of samples dried with special precautions show that in chemical composition this hay rivals bran.

SCARLET CLOVER FOR SEED PRODUCTION.

HITHERTO the demand for domestic seed has exceeded the supply. The yield of seed on properly prepared fields is noticeable. Fifteen bushels per acre have been harvested, but nine and ten bushels per acre is a large crop. Some growers attribute their success to their energy in hulling and housing their seed without losses caused by rainfalls. The large and heavy heads dry slowly if once thoroughly soaked, and the seed sprouts with remarkable rapidity. When over ripe the seed shatters easily, and a heavy percentage is thereby often wasted. Small growers have cured and housed their products and hulled it at their leisure. Others have hulled from stacks, with varying results.

SWEET CLOVER. (*Melilotus alba.*)

/

TO HULL SCARLET CLOVER SEED.

THE first consideration in this connection should be, what style of huller to use, the rasp machine or the one using spikes? Both styles have been tried a sufficient length of time to determine which is adapted to the peculiar conditions of scarlet clover In New Jersey, Delaware, Maryland and North Carolina the majority of scarlet clover fields are infested with wild onions, which are green and full of sap when the clover is cut for seed. The curing of the clover in no wise affects the onions; they are as green when they go into the machine as they were when first cut. These weeds when ground up by the huller exude a juice which oxidizes as soon as exposed to the air and forms a gum that adheres like pitch when once it becomes " set." In the spike huller this sticky substance gets into the tailings elevator and a portion of it goes through both cylinders of these machines several times, causing endless choking even in the driest of clover. The seed of scarlet clover is in a pod shaped something like a clove, and unless this pod is partially denuded of its " wings " it will lodge, point downward, in the meshes of the screen in the huller shoe and entirely fill it up. No amount of wind from the fan will dislodge them. It takes all of one man's time to keep this screen or " riddle " free from these pods, and in removing them by hand much seed is wasted. It is impossible to do good work in scarlet clover with any huller that does not demolish these pods to such a degree that they will not lodge in the "riddle."

The Birdsell rasp huller is the only machine that does this. By setting the adjustable concave to the hulling cylinder so close that only a very thin knife blade can be inserted between the rasp at the closest point and running the hulling cylinder at a speed not to exceed 750 revolutions, *with every belt on the machine well tightened*, the pods will be so ground up that they will not lodge in the "riddle," and at the same time the cylinder will clean itself of the onion gum. Should the hulling cylinder become smeared with this gum through improper adjustment, the concave can be quickly removed and with an

JAPAN CLOVER. (*Lespideza striata.*)

old broom or stiff scrubbing brush and some hot water and concentrated lye the gum is quickly removed.

Kerosene oil can be used for this in lieu of the water and lye. By exercising the proper care in the adjustment of the machine and running at the proper speed "gumming" and lodging of the seed pods will be entirely prevented with the Birdsell huller.

WHITE, OR GERMAN CLOVER.

THIS clover is too well known to need a lengthy description. It is one of the most valuable of the grasses in permanent pastures. With white clover in the dryer parts of a pasture, and alsike in the swails, or low places, in the proper proportions with other grasses, they are of inestimable value to the farmer. White clover is profitably raised for its seed in Wisconsin and in northwestern Ohio, more especially in Wisconsin. It is cut with either a mower or a scythe, and is raked up with a hand rake and either stacked or left in the field in bunches until properly cured for hulling. It is hulled successfully with a Birdsell huller only. No other machine is capable of getting and saving one-half the seed, while the Birdsell gets all of it, cleans it and sacks it in marketable condition. The yield of white clover seldom exceeds two bushels per acre, but its value in the markets fully makes up for the smaller quantity produced, as compared with red clover. The price of the white German seed is from $10 to $14 per bushel.

Besides the clovers we have mentioned in the preceding pages there are some minor clovers, the illustrations and descriptions of which we have copied, by permission, from Henry Wallace's "Clover Culture." Mr. Wallace is perhaps better informed on all that pertains to clover than any other author with whom we are acquainted. He is at present the editor and publisher of *Wallace's Farmer and Dairyman*, a weekly agricultural paper, published at Des Moines, Ia., subscription price $1 per annum. To such of our readers as desire to keep in touch with the progress of clover culture in the United States and at the same time read one of the best farm papers

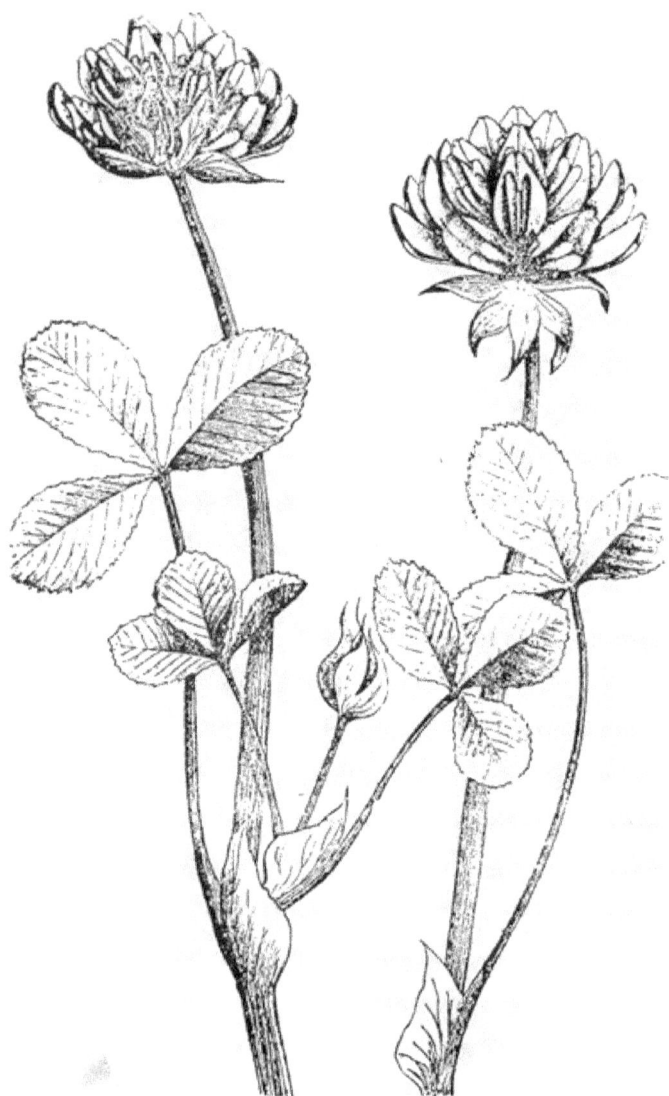

(*Trifolium fucatu m.*)

once every week, we heartily recommend *Wallace's Farmer and Dairyman*. Mr. Wallace informs us that he is now preparing a new book on the clovers fully covering all that is worth the farmer's study of the plant in all its forms, which will be given as a free premium with a year's subscription to his paper.

THE MINOR CLOVERS.

OF these is the *melilotus alba*, commonly known as sweet clover, which can be found growing in gardens, whence it escapes to the highway, vacant lots, especially in cities, and to neglected fields. A sub-variety of it is known as Bokhara clover. It grows to the height of six or eight feet on good land when not cropped, and its only value, on lands that will grow red or mammoth clover profitably, is as bee pasture. For this purpose it will pay apiarians to sow it along the roadsides or in the vacant corners and other neglected lands. In the drier portions of the west and in the south this clover has very considerable value. It is proving a valuable forage plant and also one of the renovating crops greatly needed in some of the more southern states. Trials at the Mississippi Agricultural College and by planters in that state seem to have established this fact beyond question. Like all the other clovers it has the capacity of appropriating nitrogen from the atmosphere and thus enriching the land and preparing it for the profitable production of other crops. Where it has been found impossible to grow the better varieties of clover it is worthy of trial, and experiment stations in those states where the better varieties are not a success should make a still more careful and thorough investigation of its merits.

JAPAN CLOVER.

JAPAN clover (Les Pedeza Striata). In some unknown way there was introduced a variety of clover into the south Atlantic states from Japan about forty-five years ago that has proved of no little economic value, known by the above name. It was little noticed before the late war, but during the

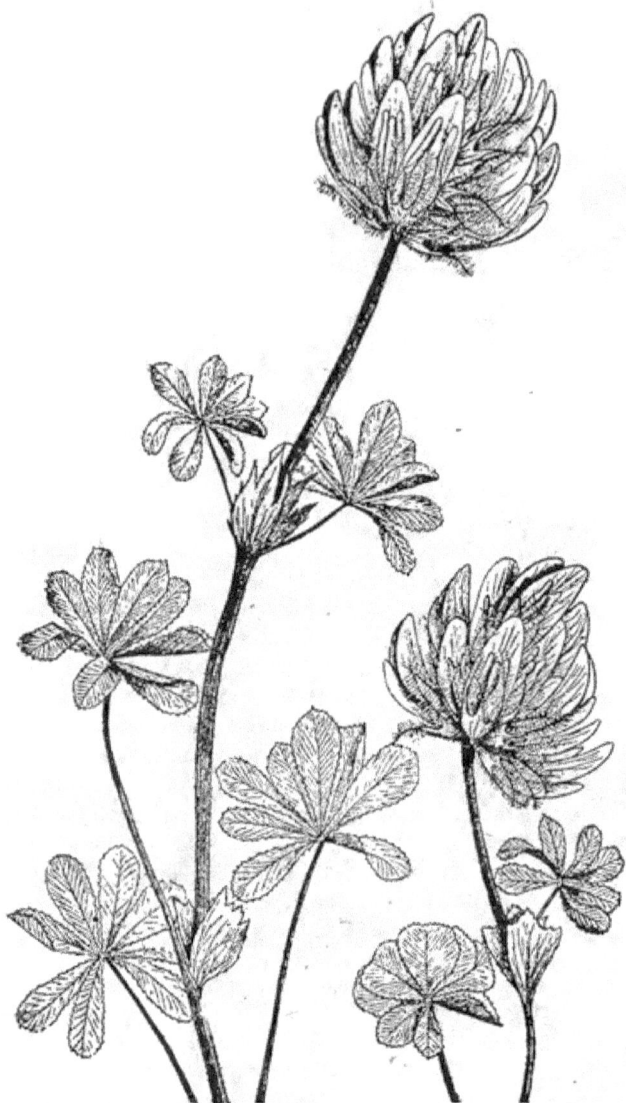

LARGE HEADED CLOVER. (*Trifolium megacephalum.*)

war it extended south and west and has spread rapidly over a large district of country, especially along roadsides, in abandoned fields and in open woods. It is an annual, growing up every spring and dying off by frost in the fall. It reproduces itself from seed on the same ground year after year. It thrives on poor soils but prefers clay, and only on rich bottom lands does it obtain size sufficient to justify cutting it for hay. It does not withstand drouth as well as Bermuda grass, but it is, nevertheless, of great value to the southern farmer. It should be sown at the rate of half a bushel to the acre.

TRIFOLIUM FUCATUM.

This is one of the largest and strongest growing of our native kinds, and is found on the Pacific coast. Under favorable circumstances it attains a height of two or three feet. The stem is decumbent, smooth, thick and juicy. The stipules at the base of the leaf are half an inch to an inch long, ovate, broad, and clasping the stem. The leaves are trifoliate, with stems or petioles three to six inches long; the leaflets vary from roundish or oblong to obovate, thickish, strongly veined, three-fourths of an inch to an inch and a half long, and with numerous small, sharp teeth on the margins. The flower heads are large (one to two inches in diameter), larger than those of the common red clover on naked peduncles (stems), which are longer than the leaf-stalks (sometimes five to six inches long). There is a conspicuous green involucre surrounding the base of the flower-head deeply divided into seven to nine ovate, entire and pointed lobes, which are about half as long as the flowers. The heads contain comparatively few flowers (about eight to ten), but these are about an inch long, thick and inflated, the calyx about one-fourth as long as the corolla, which varies from pink to purple in color. Mr. S. Watson, in the "Botany of California," says of this: "A common species in the coast ranges and in the foothills of the Sierra Nevada, through the length of the state—in some places very abundant and affording good pasturage." It would seem very desirable that this species should be given a fair trial in cultivation.

(*Trifolium involucratum.*)

TRIFOLIUM MEGACEPHALUM (Large-headed clover).

A low species, seldom reaching a foot in height, but robust and with strong, deeply penetrating roots. A number of stalks usually proceed from one root, but these stems are unbranching, somewhat hairy and terminate with a single large head. The leaves mostly proceed from the base of the stem, there usually being but one pair on the stalk near the middle. The lowest leaves are long-stalked, and with five or seven leaflets instead of three, as in most clovers, but the upper ones are sometimes reduced to three leaflets. The leaflets are an inch long or less, somewhat wedge-shaped or obovate and blunt at the apex, and with very fine, sharp teeth on the edge. The stipules at the base of the leaves are large, mostly ovate in form, and sharply toothed or deeply cut. The heads are mostly terminal, about one and one-half inches long, on a naked peduncle, and without an involucre. The flowers are large, purplish, about an inch long, and very compact and spicate in the head. The calyx with its long, plumose teeth, is half as long as the corolla. This species grows in the mountain regions of California, Oregon, Washington, Nevada and Montana. It is not as large as the common red clover, but experiments are needed to determine its possibilities for pasturage. Its large, showy heads and its peculiar leaves would make it an interesting ornamental species.

TRIFOLIUM INVOLUCRATUM.

This is an annual species, presenting a great variety of form, but under favorable circumstances reaching one and one-half or two feet in height and of vigorous growth. The stems are usually decumbent and branching below, very leafy, and terminating with one to three heads on rather long peduncles. The leaves are on stalks longer than the leaflets, which are in threes, one-half to one inch long, of an oblong or obovate form, smooth and with very fine, sharp teeth on the margins. The stipules are large, ovate, or lanceolate, and usually much gashed or deeply toothed. The heads are long-stalked, about an inch long, the purplish flowers closely

RUNNING BUFFALO CLOVER. (*Trifolium stoloniferum.*)

unded with an involucre, which is divided
g-toothed lobes. The flowers are half to three-
h long, slender, with a short, striate calyx, the
are very slender, entire and pointed, and little
the corolla. This species has a wide range of
e western part of the continent, prevailing from
British America through the mountain districts.
tivation it would probably produce a good yield of
out has never been subjected to experiment, so far as

TRIFOLIUM STOLONIFERUM (Running buffalo clover).

This is a perennial species, growing about a foot high; long
unners are sent out from the base, which are procumbent at
rst, becoming erect. The leaves are all at the base except
e pair at the upper part of the stem. The root leaves are
g-stalked, and have three thinnish obovate leaflets, which
are minutely toothed. The pair of leaves on the stem have
the stalk about as long as the leaflets, which are about one
inch long.

The stipules are ovate or lanceolate, pointed, and entire on
the margins, the lower ones nearly an inch long, the upper
ones about half as long. There are but one or two heads on
each stem at the summit, each on a peduncle longer than
the leaves. The heads are about an inch in diameter, rather
loosely flowered, each flower being on a short, slender pedicel,
or stem, which bends backward at maturity. Each flower
a long-toothed calyx about half as long as the coroll
is white tinged with purple. This species i
open woodlands and in prairies in Oh
and westward. It is smaller in
growth that the common red

cent, the stems slender, procumbent a
leaves are trifoliate, on petioles of variabl
lets are about half an inch long, obovate
base, and somewhat notched at the summit.
nearly as long as the leaflets, ovate or lanceo
toothed above. Each·stalk has usually tw
heads proceeding from the upper joints. The r
are from one-half to three-fourths of an inch in dia
out an involucre, and with numerous crowded, sm
on slender pedicels, which become reflexed in age.
lanceolate teeth of the calyx are slightly shorter t
small, purplish, pointed corolla. The pods are usuall
seeded. This species occurs in all the southern states a
Texas. It is too small to be valuable for fodder, but is wo
a trial as a constituent of pastures in the south.

THE END.

www.ingramcontent.com/pod-product-compliance
Lightning Source LLC
Chambersburg PA
CBHW031823090426

42739CB00008B/1382